## Foreword



"Our employees are our most

How often have you hea[illegible] And it's undoubtedly true - but only if they are the *right* employees for your business. Because frankly, the wrong ones are more likely to be your biggest pain in the neck...

Employing the right people is a crucial success factor for almost every organisation. The wrong employees can damage team spirit, give rise to customer complaints, taint the reputation of your business and even, in extreme cases, destroy your business altogether. That's too high a price to pay by any standards. And yet, many organisations, particularly small businesses, seem to hire the wrong people time and again. Why is that?

It all starts with the recruitment and selection process; getting it right isn't easy. It takes time and skill, and can be a frustrating undertaking. But getting it wrong at this stage will cost far more in time and money (not to mention aggravation) in the long run, so it's worth putting in the upfront effort to ensure you get the right people into your business in the first place.

In this book I look at typical mistakes that business people make when hiring new staff. I show how these mistakes can be so damaging, and what you should do instead. And I do all this without bombarding you with jargon or complicated models - I just use case studies based on my own real life experience (subtly changed to protect my sources) to illustrate the wrong approach, followed by learning points which you can easily implement in your own business.

This book is not aimed at professional HR Managers or recruitment consultants. It is not a comprehensive guide to the law on discrimination, how to write job specifications, which websites to advertise in, or how to use psychometric assessments. Rather, it provides practical guidance to ordinary business owners and managers on how to avoid some of the most common traps they would otherwise fall into when seeking new staff for their businesses.

Hiring people is always to a certain extent an act of faith; there's no absolute guarantee of success however careful you are. But you can significantly tip the odds in your favour by taking a more professional and methodical approach to the hiring process, rather than relying on "gut instinct". Let me show you how.

## CONTENTS

## Chapter 1: Knee jerk reactions

When Helen, the HR Manager, came into work that morning and saw a plain handwritten envelope on her desk, her heart sank. Somehow, she knew it was not going to be good news. And she was right. It was a resignation letter from Mike, the Call Centre Manager. In just a month, he would walk out of the door and leave the company in the lurch. Yikes! Helen reached for the phone to call the recruitment agency. Then something made her stop and take a deep breath...

Following the introduction of new technology, the company had needed fewer people in its Call Centre. Over a couple of years the team had shrunk from 18 staff to just 11, as people left and were not replaced. As a result, it had become somewhat top heavy, with both a Manager and a Supervisor looking after only nine call centre operatives.

Nevertheless Mike's letter saying he intended to take early retirement so he could spend more time with his golf clubs was a bit of a shock. Sally, the Supervisor, had never been ambitious, and had often said she was happy in her position as number two. It looked as though they would need a new Call Centre Manager.

But with the Finance Director warning of the need for cost savings, Helen had a bright idea. She went and talked to Patrick, the Head of Operations. Why not take out a layer of management, and have the Supervisors of the Call Centre and the Repairs Department reporting directly to him? Sally would be happy because her main concern was having somebody up the line to whom she could refer the really difficult callers. And the Repairs

Department already functioned perfectly well with just a Supervisor in charge.

After consultation with all the interested parties, the Operations Division was restructured accordingly. The Call Centre worked just as smoothly as before (Sally always had been the "power behind the throne" if the truth be told) and hardly ever needed to refer matters up to Patrick in practice. The customers were happy, and the company was able to make significant cost savings without any damage to its operational efficiency.

**Learning point 1**

*Whenever somebody resigns, the first question you should ask yourself is: do I* ***really*** *need to replace them? Consider how you have coped when they have been on holiday or off sick. Perhaps you can reorganize the existing team, reshuffle the duties, give some of the others a chance to take on new responsibilities, to learn and develop their skills. You may find that the rest of the team can take up the slack and you don't need to hire anybody at all.*

*Alternatively, there may be somebody more junior in the team who would relish the opportunity to step into the departing person's shoes, enabling you to hire somebody much less senior to join the team. You know your existing team's capabilities and personalities, whereas a new recruit is always something of an unknown quantity. A new person at the top of a team can potentially be more damaging if you get it wrong than a new person at a lower level, so you will be less exposed if you hire somebody further down the pecking order.*

*You may conclude that you really do need to hire on a like-for-like basis, but you should at least look at the possibility of a different solution, before picking up the phone to look for a direct replacement for the person who's leaving.*

## Chapter 2: "We need another Margaret"

Margaret was brilliant, really good at her job. She fitted in really well; everybody liked her because she was a hard worker but also a good sport who liked having a giggle with the other girls in the department. So it was a blow when her husband was offered that transfer up to Newcastle and she had to leave.

But John knew what to do. He would look for another Margaret. He dug out the advert he'd used the last time, placed it in the local paper, and sifted through the responses diligently. He was looking for a nice, steady, middle aged lady with some relevant experience and a good sense of humour, just like Margaret. No point interviewing the young lad or even the older gentleman with all the right experience – they wouldn't fit into the team.

And he found just the person. Linda seemed perfect. She had a great sense of humour, she was about the same age as Margaret - in fact she even looked a bit like her. He was sure the girls would take to her straight away.

It was a real shock to John a couple of weeks later when Gill, the team leader, came and told him that Linda wasn't working out. He couldn't understand it. Apparently Linda wasn't pulling her weight; she wasted too much time gossiping and distracting the others when they were busy. What had gone wrong?

John had assumed that because Linda reminded him of Margaret, she would turn out to have the same good qualities as she'd had. That was a mistake.

Linda didn't make it through her probationary period, and John was on the verge of re-advertising, when Gill asked to look at the CVs of the other short-listed candidates. She then suggested that actually, the young lad, Raj, seemed worth interviewing.

Luckily Raj was still looking for work so they brought him in, and Gill took part in the interview. She persuaded John to give him a chance, and within a month it was obvious that he was getting on great. In an all-female department, Raj was a hit, with his "cheeky chappy" approach, and his determination to work hard and prove himself.

**Learning Point 2**

*It's very tempting when looking for somebody to replace a successful employee, to imagine that you need a "clone" of that person. It's natural, even subconsciously, to model your expectations on what has gone before.*

*But you should resist the temptation of thinking that only somebody similar to the previous job-holder will fit the bill. However brilliant that person was, there's no reason to suppose that somebody of a different age, gender, ethnic origin, marital status or sexual orientation won't work out equally well. In fact, it's beneficial to have a variety of different types of people in a team, to provide balance and diversity – not to mention the fact that discriminating against people on the basis of age, sex, race etc. is illegal.*

*So be open-minded when looking for your next recruit. After all, it's what they can do that counts, not how closely they resemble their predecessor.*

## Chapter 3: My kind of person

Gordon's company had won the license for a new brand from the States and needed a really good Brand Manager to help launch it into the UK market. The HR Manager had given a detailed brief to the recruitment agency, and screened the candidates to arrive at a short list. Maurice seemed to tick all the boxes: he had a good track record in marketing, excellent interpersonal skills, and was clearly hard-working and determined to succeed.

As the position was so important, Gordon insisted on making the final decision – after all, he was the MD. So Maurice was invited in for one final interview. The HR Manager waited in the wings while Maurice and Gordon were ensconced in conversation. An hour and a half later, Maurice emerged, smiling, from the MD's office. Having thanked him for attending, the HR Manager went and asked Gordon what he thought.

"Yes, he's a very good chap, go ahead and make the offer".

On Maurice's first day in the new role, the HR Manager finally got the chance to ask him how the interview with Gordon had gone. What had clinched it for him?
"Well, I was expecting to be grilled about my previous experience with new brands" he said, "but once he discovered we belong to the same golf club, we spent most of the time talking about golf..."

**Learning point 3**

*It is human nature to find some people easier to get on with than others, and sometimes you just "click" with somebody straight away. And if you are going to work closely with them, it seems sensible to select people who are pleasant to be around.*

*But it can be dangerous to rely too much on instant empathy. Remember, you're looking for an employee, not a friend or a drinking buddy. You need them to be able to undertake workplace tasks which require knowledge, skills and expertise, so over-reliance on personal characteristics can be a mistake.*

*We all make initial judgments about other people very quickly – often within the first few seconds of meeting them. These judgments will be largely unconscious and based on their appearance, their body language and even (although we are generally unaware of this) their smell. Sometimes we will find ourselves saying something like: "I don't know why, but I just don't trust that person", or "I knew we'd get on the moment I laid eyes on him".*

*If a candidate is well groomed, dressed in accordance with our expectations, stands straight, looks us in the eye, has a firm dry handshake, and a genuine smile, he or she is likely to make a positive first impression before they have even said anything. Research has shown time and again that being tall, slim and physically attractive will also help a person's prospects in the workplace, as well as in life generally.*

*By contrast, somebody who turns up for an interview looking scruffy, dirty or inappropriately dressed, who slouches, avoids our gaze, has sweaty palms, and is in need of a haircut and/or a shower, will almost certainly have done him or herself no favours. Being short, physically disfigured or grossly overweight will also contribute to a poor first impression. It may not be right, but that's the way it is.*

*Once that initial judgment has been made it can be very hard to shift. If you've taken against a candidate, everything they say and do will serve to confirm your view that they are not the kind of person you want in your organisation. If on the other hand you're positively disposed towards the person, their words and actions are likely to be interpreted in a positive light. This is called the "halo and horns" effect.*

*If it then turns out that the candidate you like supports the same football team as you, or went to the same University, or there is some other common ground between you, it is very easy to get diverted from the purpose of the interview (checking out whether they can do the job or not) and spend the next twenty minutes in social chit chat. By the end of the interview, if you're not careful you may know a lot about their social pastimes and not nearly enough about their suitability for the role. But you may have convinced yourself that they are bound to be great – after all, they are so much like you!*

*All other things (skills, experience, aptitudes, work ethic etc.) being equal, then by all means offer the job to the person you like rather than the one you don't like. But first make sure that all the other things really are equal.*

*Most people believe they are good judges of character. But then, most people believe they are good drivers and good lovers too! It isn't necessarily so... A wise employer will look much deeper and take a far more professional approach when interviewing candidates for a position in their business.*

## Chapter 4: Winging it

Carolyn, the MD of a small computer hardware company, wasn't a great believer in job descriptions or prepared interview questions. She trusted her instincts; she was confident that she would recognise the right candidate when she saw them. Besides, she was so busy she didn't have time to spend hours preparing for the three sales interviews that afternoon. She'd wing it. It had always worked before...

Carolyn scanned through the CVs quickly over lunch: Terry had some pretty good sales experience, Jamilla had worked for some top companies, and Greg had attached a glowing reference from his previous manager. Any of them could probably do the job.

Carolyn started each interview with the usual questions: why had they gone into sales? What motivated them? What were their proudest achievements? After that the conversations just tended to flow. By the end of the afternoon Carolyn was confident she'd found the right candidate. Greg had been the most impressive from the start, with his smart suit and firm handshake. He had spoken eloquently about the reasons for leaving his last employer, and it was obvious they were sorry to lose him, given that brilliant reference. Carolyn picked up the phone and offered Greg the job.

Three weeks later, Carolyn was very surprised when her sales manager, Edward, expressed concerns about Greg's capabilities. This was a very technical sales position, and Greg didn't seem to be picking things up as quickly as Edward would have liked. He wasn't confident about putting together the technical quotations his customers needed, and struggled with the software.

"But he's got seven years' sales experience, and comes highly recommended by his last company!"

Edward and Carolyn looked at the paperwork again. Greg's sales experience had all been within the greetings cards sector - not the most technical of products - and the reference focused on Greg's superb interpersonal skills and loyal relationships with his customers.

Yes, Greg was a great salesperson - so long as the kind of selling required of him was based on building relationships with his customers. Faced with the need to write technical specifications and price up projects, he was out of his depth.

If Carolyn had paid more attention to the requirements of the job, and had taken the time to prepare some appropriate interview questions, she might have seen beyond the smart and personable exterior and recognised that Greg lacked the right skill set for this role.

Sadly, matters didn't improve and a month later they had to let Greg go and start again.

**Learning point 4**

*However often you've recruited, you need to approach it systematically, or you risk coming unstuck.*

*You need to create a* ***job description****, or at least check the existing one to ensure it's up to date. This should spell out in some detail the tasks and responsibilities of the role, as well as reporting lines, budgetary responsibilities and key relationships both within and outside the company.*

*Some people don't believe in job descriptions because they say roles change over time, and a new person can bring something new to the role. While both those observations may be true, remember the saying: "If you don't know what you're looking for, how will you know where to find it?"*

*Job descriptions can never be 100% exhaustive and a job holder may well have additional abilities that are useful to the business, but that's all the more reason to take time to identify the* **core** *elements of the role, particularly its principal objectives – the reasons why it exists in the first place - rather than just creating a list of tasks which may become out of date.*

*From that, you can derive a* ***person specification*** *that highlights the essential knowledge, skills, experience and qualifications needed for success in the job. Avoid any potentially discriminatory requirements like gender, age, etc.*

*These documents will form the basis of your advertisement, or the briefing document for your recruitment agency if you are using one.*

*Then, when you have the candidates' CVs in front of you, draw up some* ***probing interview questions*** *designed to get into the nitty-gritty detail of their previous experience, asking for specific examples of how they handled situations they are likely to come across in this job.*

*You may even devise a short* ***work-related exercise*** *for the candidates, to test to what extent they are able to put their skills and abilities into practice.*

*Finally, if you can, get somebody else to* ***conduct the final interviews with you****, so you can compare your respective perceptions of each candidate, to ensure you make the right decision.*

*Relying on gut instinct is a bad idea! Remember the old adage: "If you fail to plan, you plan to fail".*

## Chapter 5: Great advert - shame about the package

Lawrence's departure after so many years with the Company had taken everybody by surprise. They had treated him more or less as part of the furniture! He'd worked his way up over the years from a very junior position in the Accounts department all the way to Financial Controller. He'd dealt with the auditors, carried out credit control, done the forecasts and budgets – basically he'd been responsible for everything to do with finance.

Nevertheless every cloud has a silver lining and the Company saw it as an opportunity to get "new blood" into the place; a fresh pair of eyes to look at how things were being done and perhaps suggest ways of doing them better. They tasked Bethany, the Directors' PA, with the job of advertising the role and screening the applicants before the General Manager, Bernard, interviewed the shortlisted candidates.

Bethany understood the importance of preparing properly before advertising a role. She knew that she needed to prepare a detailed job description and a person specification from which she could then draft a very specific advert. She knew that the Company wanted somebody professionally qualified and with experience in their business sector. She also knew that the Company was looking for bottom line improvements so she specified in the advert that the successful candidate would need a proven track record in cost reduction measures. She topped and tailed the advert with the salary and location, some blurb about the Company, and details of how to apply, and placed the advert on a specialist online recruitment website.

She expected to be swamped with applications but in fact she only got 35 responses to the advert. She wasn't sure whether to be relieved or disappointed. But she told herself that it was better to receive 35 applications from people who fitted the bill, than 350 from time wasters.

She went through the CVs methodically and whittled them down to the four strongest contenders. To be honest, none of them ticked every single box: a couple had good experience and qualifications but not in the right sector, one had sector experience but not at a senior level, and one was well-qualified but couldn't demonstrate the cost reductions they were interested in. Nevertheless she put them forward to Bernard, who proceeded to interview them all.

When he'd finished, he called Bethany into his office and told her that he hadn't been convinced that any of the candidates was quite what he was looking for. Together, they looked at the advert again, to work out what was wrong with it. The job content and person specification seemed fine, and the website where it had been placed was spot on. So what else could explain the lack of success? Bernard was busy so he asked Bethany to figure it out.

As she drove home that evening, a thought occurred to her. Was the package on offer appropriate for the level of person they were looking for? She had accepted without question the directive that she should offer no more than they'd been paying Lawrence. Perhaps that was not enough to attract the calibre of candidates

Bernard had in mind? She decided to do a bit of digging...

The following afternoon, Bethany went back to see Bernard with the results of her research. To attract individuals with the qualifications and depth of experience the Company needed, they would have to increase the salary by around 15%. It had become clear to her that Lawrence had been significantly underpaid for what he did – probably because he had been with the Company for so many years he didn't realise his own worth, and also the fact that he lived within walking distance of the office meant that what the job lacked in financial rewards it made up for in convenience.

She put her case convincingly enough that, despite his initial reservations, Bernard reluctantly agreed to let her re-advertise the role on the higher salary. Sure enough, second time round the calibre of applicants was significantly higher, and they were able to make an offer to the right person.

**Learning Point 5**

*There is no point specifying in minute detail exactly what kind of Rolls Royce you want to buy, if you only have the budget for a Mini. All aspects of the offering need to be right, and that includes the remuneration package.*

*Figuring out the "going rate" for the job in your industry and in your part of the country is no longer a difficult or expensive undertaking; the Internet is a great tool for finding out what other comparable organisations are offering, and there are free online salary surveys which you can look at. Some recruitment agencies also publish data on average salaries for different types of role. So it's worth doing that extra bit of research to ensure you are offering a package that is competitive enough to attract the right candidates.*

*If you then find that your budget won't stretch to accommodate everything you want, you will have to compromise somewhere along the line. Maybe you could look for a person with potential rather than experience – if you do this you will be committing yourself to spending more time training that person, but it may be a worthwhile investment. Or perhaps you could consider whether the role could be done on a part time basis enabling you to reduce the salary accordingly. Or perhaps you could offer some non-financial perks to attract the right candidates without breaking the bank, such as flexible working hours.*

*Whatever you do, there's no way of getting a quart out of a pint pot, so don't waste time trying.*

## Chapter 6: Motor Mouth

Diane was an excellent salesperson and was very proud of how far she'd come since her early days in telesales all those years ago. She'd risen through the ranks by dint of hard work, enthusiasm, and a facility for talking her way out of pretty much every situation she'd ever come across, in order to get what she wanted. She was a hit with the customers and a role model for the team of salespeople she was now in charge of since her promotion to Sales Manager.

So when Connor, the MD, asked her to recruit another person to join the expanding sales team, she was confident she could handle it. If *she* couldn't spot a good salesperson when she saw one, no-one could!

Writing the advert was a positive pleasure, it allowed her to wax lyrical about the amazing growth the company was experiencing, the fantastic opportunities to earn uncapped commission, and the first class training available to get the new recruit up and running. By the time she'd finished, the job sounded irresistible!

Diane was thrilled with the responses she received: her email Inbox was flooded every day with hopeful applicants by the dozen. By the time the deadline for applications closed, she'd received over 300 CVs!

By burning the midnight oil, she whittled them down to the most promising 12 to invite for interview, and scheduled them in for an hour each over the course of 2 days, back to back.

By the end of day two she was exhausted, but really pumped up. She'd thoroughly enjoyed talking to them all: telling them about the company and its products - which were the best in the marketplace - and about their prospects for success, how good the package was, the way she liked to manage people, and how supportive the rest of the team would be.

The hard part was deciding how to select the best three to meet the MD at the second round stage. She pulled out the CVs again and tried to focus her thoughts. That guy with the red tie and highly polished shoes... was it Ricky or Robbie? He'd been very impressive. And then there was the tall woman with the glossy black hair and smart suit. Sam, was it - or Sue?

After much pencil chewing, Diane arrived at her short list and presented it to Connor. He perused them for a while and then asked her to provide a short summary on each candidate, to supplement the information on the CVs. What had it been in particular that she'd liked about them? What questions had she asked them, and how had their answers stood out from the crowd?

Diane mumbled a few platitudes before her mind went blank and her face went bright red, as she struggled to remember what it was they'd said that had impressed her. Under the MD's penetrating gaze, for once, her legendary "gift of the gab" deserted her.

Connor, who knew how enthusiastic and expressive Diane was, quickly guessed the truth. Diane had spent far too much of the time at every interview *talking to* the candidates, and not enough time *listening to* them.

She'd been so keen to "sell the job" that she hadn't given them a chance properly to sell themselves. There'd been a lot of nodding and smiling from the candidates, and they'd all looked very smart, so she'd warmed to them; but when she was put on the spot she couldn't honestly claim to have followed a rigorous line of questioning or probed their initial responses to test them out.

Connor decided he'd have to get more involved in the process himself, and sent Diane off to get all 12 shortlisted candidates' CVs so that he could make his own mind up.

## Learning Point 6

*In an interview situation, the candidate should do at least two thirds of the talking. Remember the saying: "You have two ears and one mouth, so you should do twice as much listening as talking".*

*A good way to structure an interview can be remembered using the acronym WASP:*

- *Welcome*
- *Ask Questions*
- *Supply Information*
- *Part Company*

*Structured in that way, you can make sure that the candidate's answers cannot be influenced by the information that has already been provided, thus reducing the risk of them simply saying what they know you want to hear!*

*Set a time limit for the interview and plan to spend about two thirds of it on the "welcome and ask questions" part of it. Then prepare appropriate questions beforehand, to ensure you get the information you need to supplement your initial impressions.*

*After that, invite your candidate to ask questions of their own, give them any important information about the job and the company, and advise them what the next steps will be before they leave.*

## Chapter 7: Nosey Parker

Emma was a real "people person"; she loved talking to people and finding out all about them. She believed that the key to managing staff was to really get to know them, to really understand what made them tick. And she knew that the way to do that was to ask questions – lots of questions.

Knowing how friendly and interested she was, when the Office Manager unexpectedly went off sick right in the middle of recruiting for a new Receptionist, the MD, Trevor, asked Emma to conduct the first round interviews. The invitations had already been sent to the candidates, and all Emma needed to do was to meet them all, find out a bit about them, tell them about the company, and put the best three forward.

She took it all very seriously. She knew she would have to start by putting them all at their ease, because interviews were stressful. She knew she should ask a lot of questions to find out whether they had the right skills and would fit into the company and project the appropriate image on Reception. And she knew that she should give them a chance to ask questions of their own, before wrapping up by explaining what would happen next. Oh yes, Emma was nothing if not organised!

She decided to ask all the candidates the same set of questions for consistency, and make notes of their answers. She would also jot down her impressions about their appearance, communication skills and other important personal attributes. She typed up all her prepared questions and printed out six copies of the document, one for each candidate. She was very pleased with her preparation for the interviews.

Emma stuck faithfully to her plans. True, each interview did last for two hours, but then she was determined to ensure every candidate had the opportunity to give a full account of him or herself. And of course, once she met each candidate and started talking to them, other questions occurred to her that were particularly relevant to them as individuals, so she asked those too.

It was exhausting but by the end of the process she was very clear about which three candidates to put forward for the final round.

When Trevor called Emma into his office a week later, she was expecting to be congratulated for her thoroughness. Nothing could have prepared her for what happened next.

"I'm afraid we have had letters of complaint from two of the candidates you interviewed last week. One of them says that you asked intrusive questions about her nationality and English language skills. She says that because she has an Asian name you assumed she wasn't British and asked her where she came from. You also asked whether she was married, what ages her children were, and who looked after them when she was at work!

"The other candidate is threatening to take legal action against us, because you asked a lot of questions about his age, medical background, and how much time he'd had off sick in the last five years – just because he was using a walking stick.

What on earth were you thinking, asking those sorts of questions?"

Emma was dumbfounded. Wasn't it obvious why she had asked those questions? She started to explain her rationale.

"Well, I know that people must have the right to work in the UK so as that candidate was Asian I wanted to find out what nationality she was and whether English was her first language. Over the phone people need to be able to understand..."

But she never got the chance to finish. Trevor stood up and was clearly exasperated. "Stop right there! Haven't you heard about unlawful discrimination?"

Emma was so stunned she didn't know what to say. She just sat and stared as he carried on talking.

"There are certain questions you just can't ask! You can't ask people what nationality they are, or what childcare arrangements they've got in place, or about their medical history. Those questions could land the company in deep trouble."

At that point, Trevor caught her wounded expression and his tone softened a little.

"Emma, I know you meant well, but you have to be careful how you phrase things. If you want to establish whether a person has the right to work in the UK, then that's the question to ask – and ask it of everybody, not just the candidates who look or sound foreign. There are plenty of British Asians, you know, who were born and bred here, and speak English just as well as anybody else. You can judge candidates' verbal communication skills by listening to how they express themselves during the interview.

"If you want to know whether they can work overtime, you should ask them whether they have any commitments that prevent them from working extra hours, not about what arrangements they have in place for childcare. You mustn't make assumptions based on a person's gender, marital status, family circumstances or age. I mean, would you ask somebody at interview whether they were gay or straight?"

"No, of course not!" Emma exclaimed. "That's got nothing to do with their ability to do the job, has it?"

"Precisely my point!" Trevor smiled. "All you need to ask at interview is stuff that's relevant to whether the candidate can do the job. And phrase it in the right way, so that nobody can take offence or feel you're singling them out on account of some unconscious prejudice or other."

From Emma's face, Trevor realised that the penny had dropped. If she did any interviewing in future, she wouldn't make the same mistakes again. And he'd make sure she got some proper training first, too.

**Learning Point 7**

*It is very important, when conducting a recruitment interview, to ask the **right** questions. It is a very good idea to prepare questions beforehand, and to be consistent, asking the same set of core questions to each candidate.*

*Good questioning technique is a skill that can be learned, and that improves with practice.*

- *To get a candidate to open up, it is useful to use **open** questions, such as "Tell me about…" or "Describe a time when…"*
- ***Probing** questions help you gain a deeper understanding, e.g. "How exactly did you…?"*
- *And **closed** questions will establish specific facts and bring a line of questioning to a close, like "How many people reported directly to you?" or "When did you leave?"*

*But it is important to pay attention not just to the question type but also to the **content** of the question, and to be aware of any unconscious assumptions you may be making when choosing to ask a particular candidate a particular question. Here's why.*

*There are nine "protected characteristics" under The Equality Act 2010: age, race/nationality, gender, marital status, pregnancy/maternity, disability, sexual orientation, religion or belief, and gender reassignment (sex change). So steer clear of any questions that might be interpreted as discriminating against people on any of those grounds.*

*You may have had no intention whatsoever of treating people unfairly on account of their age, gender, religion or whatever, but they may interpret your questions as discriminatory, and if they don't get the job, they may well decide to make allegations of unlawful discrimination against you. Remember, they don't need to be employees to take your company to an Employment Tribunal – candidates can do so too.*

*So if you are about to ask a woman about her family commitments or childcare arrangements, or plans to start a family,* ***don't****! You would almost certainly be demonstrating gender bias. Men don't get asked that sort of question...*

*If it's not relevant to the person's ability to do the job, then it's not a question you should ask. Even if what you are seeking to find out is legitimate and relevant, you need to be careful how you phrase it.*

*Steer clear of asking about people's religious beliefs or practices. If your job requires a candidate to work on Fridays or Sundays, don't ask whether they are practising Jews or Christians; ask whether they are happy to work on Fridays or Sundays. If they say yes, that's all you need to know.*

## Chapter 8: "I don't like to be rushed..."

Robert was a cautious character, he was always wary about rushing into things. He realised that hiring a new team member was a very important step to take and didn't want to make a mistake. For this reason he decided to take a very methodical approach to the whole process.

He drafted a job description and a person specification, wrote a very detailed job advert, and planned his interview strategy. He researched the best websites before placing the advert, and was very pleased with the response he received. He waited for a couple of weeks just in case the ideal candidate might be on vacation (it was August after all) and then got a trusted colleague, Mark, to review all the CVs with him.

They reviewed them all independently and then compared their respective shortlists. They sorted the CVs into three piles, a "Yes" pile to invite for interview straight away (the ones they both agreed on), a "Maybe" pile to keep in reserve (the ones only one of them was keen to see) and a "No" pile of candidates that neither of them thought would fit the bill. Robert felt sure that, after all this care and attention, he would find the ideal candidate.

He took the same methodical approach to the interview process itself. He arranged to see six people altogether, three on Tuesday and the other three on Thursday. He asked each person the same set of prepared questions for consistency, as well as some questions specific to each individual, based on the particulars of their CV. He wrote notes after each interview to ensure he didn't forget who had said what.

He knew it would be foolish to make a decision there and then so he and his colleague Mark had a discussion on Friday and compared their impressions of the six candidates they had seen.

Unfortunately, their views did not match. Robert favoured Barbara whereas Mark thought Imogen was a stronger candidate. Robert decided to sleep on it.

On his way in to work the following Monday, Robert turned matters over and over in his mind. As he and Mark didn't agree, maybe the right candidate hadn't been seen yet. He looked at all the CVs again. He spotted a couple in the "Maybe" pile and decided to interview them as well. He didn't want to overlook potentially suitable candidates. He saw them on the Friday but they didn't really pass muster, so it was back to square one.

Robert decided to arrange second round interviews. Unfortunately one of his three shortlisted candidates was away for a week which delayed matters somewhat. But the good news was that after the second interviews, he and Mark were in agreement: Barbara was the best candidate.

Then Robert started having doubts about the package. They had budgeted for £25k plus a bonus, but perhaps they should offer her less at first to give themselves scope for a pay rise after six months. Would she accept £23k to start with? Robert decided to do a bit more research into the "going rate" for the job. And he thought he'd better check with his accountant that the business could really afford to pay that salary. After all, now that he'd found the right candidate, he didn't want to risk offering the wrong package…

Once he had heard back from the accountant, Robert called Barbara, told her how impressed he had been, and offered her the job.

"Thank you so much, Robert" she said, "that's really flattering, but I'm afraid I've already accepted another offer. You see, I'd been to see the other company the week before my second interview with you, and when I didn't hear from you straight away I thought I couldn't keep them waiting any longer. I'm starting there on Monday."

**Learning Point 8**

*Careful preparation is important, and involving somebody else in the decision making process can be very useful. You need to invest time and effort up front in determining what you want, devising a good advert, and conducting your interviews well. And it is never a good idea to make an offer to a candidate if you are not entirely sure they are right for your business and your job.*

*However, the advent of the Internet and email has meant that the whole recruitment process has speeded up significantly. Your candidates may go home after their interview with you and find dozens of alternative roles sitting in their email Inbox. Some of those roles may seem more attractive than yours. Regardless of the state of the economy, the best people will always be in demand.*

*So once you have identified the right candidate, you need to contact them straight away, before somebody else has the chance to snap them up. If you dither, you will lose out.*

## Chapter 9: The right experience

Daniel was a great believer in experience. He had little time for all those "Smart-Alecs" with business degrees. He had worked his way up the ranks to his current position within ASG Holdings and thought there was no substitute for hard graft and experience "at the sharp end". He knew exactly what he wanted: somebody with at least ten years' experience in an organisation in the same sector, so that's what he stipulated in the advert.

When the CVs came in, he was disappointed to find there was only one candidate who actually had the sort of experience he was looking for. He didn't like the idea of having only one person to choose from. He mentioned it to Olivia, the Office Manager, when they met at the coffee machine. She was a sensible woman and he trusted her judgment.

Olivia offered to have a look at the CVs, and pulled out a couple that Daniel had discarded. "But they haven't got enough experience!" he protested "And they've worked in completely different businesses to ours".

Olivia explained her rationale. It was true that they didn't have ten years' worth of experience because they were relatively young, but they'd been promoted rapidly through their organisations and were responsible for some quite high level projects. The organisations they'd worked for, albeit not in the same sector, were household names renowned for providing good quality training. Plus, both candidates had strong academic credentials and were likely to be fast learners.

Daniel decided he had nothing to lose by interviewing these two alongside his favoured candidate. He asked Olivia if she'd be prepared to sit in on the interviews with him, even though deep down he was pretty sure he'd go for the experienced candidate.

To his surprise, one of the youngsters, Ben, really stood out. Not only was he intelligent and articulate, he also demonstrated real enthusiasm and a willingness to knuckle down and work hard. What he lacked in experience he made up for with his other qualities.

Olivia expressed it very well: "Ben may have less experience, but he has more *potential* than either of the others" she said. "He'll be up to speed within a few months and then he'll really come into his own."

Daniel realised that all he needed to do was to teach Ben how things were done in ASG Holdings, and he would quickly pick up the baton and run with it. And that's exactly what happened. Ben soon proved himself to be a real asset to Daniel's department – even without ten years' experience.

**Learning Point 9**

*When you have a vacancy to fill it's tempting to look for somebody who has "done it all before". But experience alone doesn't guarantee success. In fact, sometimes a person who has done the same thing somewhere else will have developed some bad habits along the way, or may be slow to adapt to your ways, continually harking back to "how we used to do it in my last company"...*

*Furthermore, if they have done it all before, they are unlikely to find your job much of a challenge and may get bored fairly quickly, or may feel they can "coast along" and not try too hard because they know it all already.*

*A candidate with the right attitude, aptitudes and potential can actually be keener to learn and make an impact, and ultimately prove more successful, than one with more experience.*

## Chapter 10: He came highly recommended!

Derek was thrilled to bits with the results of his recruitment campaign. He'd really been thorough; he'd specified exactly what the job entailed and what kind of person he'd need to fill it. The advert had been very detailed, spelling out exactly what skills, qualifications and experience would be needed for success. He'd sifted the CVs carefully and rejected all the candidates who didn't fit the criteria.

At interview, it was clear that his attention to detail had paid off. He had three excellent candidates, all of whom had the necessary qualifications, and it was difficult to choose between them. In the end he plumped for Sanjay, who was very personable and gave a great account of himself, and who had been proactive enough to supply a reference from his last employer before even being asked. He'd also got a First Class Honours degree in Information Technology. Derek felt sure he would be an asset to the organisation.

When he first noticed Sanjay making silly little mistakes, Derek put it down to "teething problems". He'd settle down soon enough, he was probably just nervous. It's always strange when you first join a new company...

But after a while people started to complain. Sanjay didn't seem to know some pretty basic stuff that should have been second nature to somebody with his experience and qualifications. Derek was puzzled. On paper Sanjay ticked all the boxes, but in practice something wasn't right.

Over dinner with friends one Friday evening, he described the situation to his wife's friend Rosie, who was in recruitment.

"Did you check his references and qualifications?" she asked.

"Oh yes, he supplied an excellent reference; his previous employer thought very highly of him! And he's got a First in IT from a very good university." Derek replied.

"No, I mean, did you *check* them? Did you contact his previous company and talk to his manager? And did you ask to see his degree certificate so you could take a copy for your records?"

Derek had to admit that he had not actually checked; he had taken it all at face value.

On Monday he phoned Sanjay's previous company and asked to speak to his old boss, Harry Jones. The receptionist hesitated and then said: "We don't have anybody here by that name." Derek was put through to the HR Manager, who confirmed that Sanjay had worked there, but only for six months, and had been dismissed at the end of his probationary period for failing to live up to expectations.

It was the same story when Derek contacted the University. Sanjay had started the IT course but had failed to complete it; he didn't have a degree at all, let alone a First Class one.

When confronted with these facts, Sanjay confessed that he had typed the reference himself on a piece of letterhead he had purloined from his previous employer, inventing the manager's name and getting a friend to sign it. And he had also lied about his qualifications.

He realised the game was up and agreed to leave immediately.

**Learning Point 10**

*You know the old adage: "The job's not finished until the paperwork's done" – well it applies to recruitment too. Even once the person's on board, your job is not finished. You need to check references – which can involve contacting previous employers to ensure that the person whose name you have been given is a bona fide referee and not the person's friend or partner.*

*Often nowadays references will be short and to the point, merely confirming the dates of employment and the person's job title upon departure, but even that information can be useful. Check that the dates provided match those on the candidate's CV; if they don't then you will have cause for concern about the veracity of the CV itself.*

*And if qualifications are crucial for the job, ask to see the original certificates and take a copy for the file. It's not difficult to download fake qualifications from the Internet, or mock up something on a computer, so insist on seeing the originals, and if in doubt, make further inquiries. Research suggests that up to 40% of CVs are not entirely truthful, so don't take it all at face value.*

## Chapter 11: "What do you mean, he's not Spanish?"

Arthur might not be in his first flush of youth, but he prided himself on his open-minded, liberal approach. He wasn't one of those crusty old curmudgeons who never stopped harping back to some golden age when Britannia ruled the waves, and people ate pie and mash, not Chicken Tikka Masala. He liked a good curry, as it happened.

As for all the concerns about immigration, well, he wasn't prejudiced against foreigners. As long as they worked hard, paid their taxes, and could understand English well enough to do their jobs, he didn't mind where they'd come from or what colour they were. His logistics company was multi-cultural all right, but they all got on well and didn't give him any grief. What more could a manager ask for?

Take Juan, for example, that nice young Spaniard who'd joined about eighteen months ago. He didn't say much, but he got on with the job, worked hard, always volunteered for overtime when it was offered. Quite honestly, if all the workers in the company were as good as him, Arthur wouldn't have minded if they'd all come over from Bilbao, or wherever it was.

So when Arthur answered the phone one Friday afternoon and heard a heavily disguised voice telling him to watch out because he was employing an illegal immigrant, he thought it was just a sick joke. How ridiculous! Everybody in the place was British or came from somewhere in the EU. There were some nasty right wing types in that area. He decided to take no notice.

The following week an envelope came in the post, marked "Private and Confidential". It contained an anonymous typed note repeating the warning that the company would get into trouble because it employed illegal immigrants. He felt a bit of a knot form in his stomach. Could there be some truth in this?

He decided to do something about it, if only to set his mind at rest. That evening he went online and searched for information about illegal workers. He found the UK Border Agency website and read up about an employer's obligations. Apparently he was supposed to have checked everybody's immigration status when he first employed them, and if he did happen to be employing an illegal immigrant the company could be fined up to £20,000!

Well, that clinched it. He'd get the entire workforce to provide the relevant documentation to settle matters once and for all. They might grumble, but that was too bad.

At the toolkit talk that Monday morning he told them all that they needed to bring in their passports. It was just a formality, he reassured them, just a bit of bureaucracy. But he was confident they could easily comply - I mean, who doesn't have a passport these days?

The next day Arthur spent several hours taking photocopies of everybody's documentation. But Juan didn't turn up for work that day, he phoned in sick. He'd never missed a day's work before. How odd!

Arthur never saw Juan again. He just seemed to disappear without a trace; he wasn't answering his phone or responding to any letters. Arthur couldn't understand it.

One day he saw Miguel and called him over. Perhaps he knew something; they'd been great mates, often jabbering away in Spanish during their breaks.

Miguel looked sheepish, he really didn't want to talk, but Arthur could tell he knew something. Arthur had to drag it out of him.

"Juan wasn't Spanish" he said. "He was from Bolivia. He came to the UK on a student visa and never went back. He said there was no work back home. He was sending money to his mother every month. Then when you asked for passports, he was afraid you would report him, so he left. I don't know where he's gone, but I don't think he's in this city any more."

**Learning Point 11**

*Employers must never take a person's nationality at face value, whatever their skin colour, accent or appearance. Even a person who looks and sounds like a native Brit needs to be checked to ensure they have the right to work in the UK. Every employment is conditional on the person having that right, and if they don't then the contract is null and void.*

*The fact is that employing an illegal worker can get your company into a lot of trouble. It really is vital to carry out proper immigration checks on all new recruits before they start working for you.*

*The easiest way to do this is to ask to see an original passport when the person comes along for their final interview – don't accept a photocopy in case it's been doctored – and take a copy of the front cover and the photo page for your records. If the passport is British or from the EU or another EEA country (like Switzerland) then the person has the unfettered right to work here and that's all you need to do.*

*If it's a passport from another country, or if the person doesn't have a passport, you will find a list of other acceptable documents on the UKBA website. If you are in any doubt as to the validity of any of the documents you see, make further checks.*

*Finally, if you have taken a copy of a passport from a candidate you don't end up hiring for any reason, destroy it within a reasonable period of time, as it contains personal data under the Data Protection Act.*

## Chapter 12: This is just the beginning

Jeremy had been so relieved when he'd received Vanessa's signed contract confirming she'd join him on the first of July. At last, he could put the whole time-consuming recruitment exercise behind him and get on with the "day job"!

So he was devastated when Vanessa came to see him after only 3 weeks in post, saying that she'd made a mistake when she'd joined Fullwood Engineering, and was handing in her notice. What on earth had gone wrong?

Vanessa was obviously the ideal candidate for the role. She had all the skills and experience required, and she was a smiley, charming person whom everybody instantly liked. Jeremy had realised how important it was to snap her up quickly before some other employer had the chance. So he'd phoned her first thing on the morning after the interview and said she could start the following Monday.

Admittedly, the team leader Susan was on holiday at the time, but the other girls would make Vanessa feel welcome, surely. It wouldn't be a problem.

On her first morning, Vanessa had turned up and asked for Jeremy because he hadn't told her the name of her line manager. He'd been in a meeting so the receptionist had asked Vanessa to wait until he was free. She'd been there for about an hour and a half before Jeremy had come down to me greet her. But he'd been profusely apologetic, and she'd said it was all right.

When they'd got upstairs to the department, he'd found her a desk and asked one of the others to show her where everything was – the toilets, the coffee machine, etc. The IT department had organised a computer for her on Wednesday, although admittedly it wasn't connected to the system for another couple of days and there'd been that mix up over the passwords... but it was all sorted out by the end of the week.

Vanessa had asked for a written contract of employment, and he'd said he'd see to it, but he'd been terribly busy and it really wasn't all that important, was it? Just some bureaucratic nonsense that could wait until Susan came back and completed the forms for the payroll department. As for a Staff Handbook, he'd dug out a copy for her, albeit it was a bit out of date...

When her first salary payment had been wrong because they'd had to use an emergency tax code, Jeremy had personally gone and apologised to Vanessa, and authorised a cheque to be issued to make up the difference.

Basically, he'd bent over backwards to resolve all the teething problems that had arisen. And now she was sitting there in front of him, saying she was going to leave! But why? Where was she going?

Vanessa clearly felt uncomfortable explaining her decision, but Jeremy persisted. In the end she said:

"I'm afraid I just don't think this is my kind of company. You see, I'm an organised person, I like to plan everything, dot all the i's and cross all the t's. Since I've been here, I've got the impression that things are done, well, a bit "on the hoof". It's like, nobody was really expecting me to turn up, and nothing was ready. I still haven't had my contract.

"The other company that interviewed me around the same time as Fullwood Engineering has already sent me a Welcome Pack, including a personal details form, a copy of the Staff Handbook, a telephone list - everything. I just think I'll feel more comfortable in that kind of environment."

Jeremy hung his head. She was absolutely right; they hadn't got things ready for her. It had all been incredibly slapdash.

**Learning Point 12**

*Recruitment doesn't end when the person has accepted the job offer; in some ways that's just the beginning.*

*First impressions work both ways. When somebody new joins your organisation; they need to impress you, but you also need to impress them. You need to make them feel welcome so they will settle in quickly.*

*As soon as your offer of employment is accepted you need to set the wheels in motion to prepare for their arrival. Organising their desk, computer, password, induction training, contract of employment, telephone lists, introductions around the office etc. are all part of the process.*

*The first few months of a new person's tenure are the time when they are most at risk of leaving, either of their own volition or because you decide they are not working out. If you are happy that you've made the right decision in hiring that person, it's up to you to make sure they don't change their mind before you've had a chance to get any return on the investment you have made in recruiting them.*

*It is natural that a new person will feel like a fish out of water at first, but if you take an organised approach to their first few weeks, it will help them feel at home and start to build successful working relationships.*

## Chapter 13: Give it time...

Sometimes, with the best will in the world, you end up compromising, Cecil thought, as he looked at the department's performance statistics. His need for an extra person had been so urgent that he'd offered the job to Valerie despite some initial misgivings. He'd invested heavily in her: he'd sent her on training courses, bought new computer equipment, and dedicated lots of management time to getting her up and running... He was determined it was going to work out. Failure was not an option.

When he started hearing mutterings that Valerie wasn't cutting the mustard, he ignored them. It was early days. She needed time to adjust to the new way of doing things – after all, she'd been with her last company for 18 years, it was bound to be unsettling for her. She'd find her feet.

Then she broke her wrist and couldn't drive for two weeks. When she came back, the Fit Note said she had to be careful not to do too much on the computer while her wrist was still in the sling, and she shouldn't lift anything until it was properly healed. Well, it could happen to anyone, it was not her fault, and it wouldn't be fair to judge her performance until she was completely better.

When one of her colleagues complained that Valerie wasn't pulling her weight, Cecil pointed out that she'd got to be careful as her wrist was still weak. "Give her time; she'll get up to speed" he said.

When her husband had an accident and Valerie had to drop everything and rush to the hospital, it really shook her up; for weeks afterwards she would get tearful if anybody said anything. Well, she was very sensitive. She'd get back to normal eventually.

At the end of her six month probationary period, she hadn't made as much progress as Cecil would have liked, but she'd had a run of back luck, hadn't she? And the department was so stretched they couldn't manage if she wasn't there, so he decided to confirm her appointment. Things would get better.

And so it went on. There were always plausible explanations why Valerie's performance wasn't really as good as the others, why her attendance was a bit worse than that of her peers, or why the others in her team didn't really get on with her.

Before he knew it, Valerie had been with the company for a couple of years. He had to concede that she was a bit of a weak link, but she never did anything drastically wrong, so he couldn't really justify taking any remedial action...

One day he was in philosophical mood at the bowling club, and shared his frustrations with his good friend Albert. What he said took Cecil by surprise.

"You know your trouble, Cecil? You're just too nice for your own good. Surely Valerie just isn't good enough? Are you being fair on your other employees by keeping her on? Are you being fair on your customers? Doesn't your business deserve better?"

**Learning Point 13**

*The purpose of a probationary period is to assess whether you have made a good, bad or indifferent hiring decision. If you have any concerns about a new recruit, this is the time to tackle them. Obviously people will need some time to settle in, and there will be a learning curve at the beginning. And everybody does get sick occasionally. But if you still have doubts about a person's suitability after six months, the chances are that person is not right for your business, and you should cut your losses sooner rather than later.*

*By being too patient, making too many excuses, or just being reluctant to grasp the nettle and admit that you got it wrong, you are not doing your business justice. By tolerating below par performance in the hope that things will simply improve by themselves, you risk filling your business with mediocre employees. Your customers deserve better than that.*

*Start as you mean to carry on, by setting objective realistic criteria for judging a new recruit during the probationary period, e.g. reaching a certain level of output, or mastering a certain key task. Have a clear written plan for training and supporting the person through the initial learning curve, and make sure it is implemented. Have regular meetings to ensure they are making the anticipated progress and give both parties a chance to discuss any areas of concern.*

*As the end of the probatonary period approaches, review their performance against your criteria. If it's not good enough, either extend the probationary period for another month or two with a very clear message that improvement is necessary (and be prepared to do something about it, like provide more training or coaching), or dispense with their services at that stage.*

*Depending on what it says in your contract, you may be able to bypass the usual performance management or disciplinary procedures and simply dismiss with a week's notice. It's possible that some of the other candidates you interviewed may still be available, so if you had a strong second choice candidate, get in touch and find out. With luck you won't even have to go through a full-blown recruitment procedure to find a replacement.*

*Just "giving it time" is seldom a good strategy if a new recruit is not working out. Be fair to the person, of course, but if it becomes clear that you made a poor hiring decision, cut your losses sooner rather than later, and start again.*

## Chapter 14: "But he gets results!"

Tom was in many ways an excellent hire – he was hard working and clever and learned the nuts and bolts of the job very quickly. He was undoubtedly highly intelligent (he'd studied Maths at Cambridge) and mastered the IT systems without any difficulty. And he delivered results. Yes, thought Doug, the team leader, an intellectual heavy weight with a good work ethic was just what they needed...

But beneath the surface there were mutterings. People didn't seem to enjoy working with Tom. Everybody seemed so much more cheerful when he wasn't around.

When Charlotte asked for a quiet word with the Office Manager, alarm bells started to ring. Charlotte had been there for five years and was a well-respected and high-performing administrator, but she was asking for a transfer to another department, just to get away from Tom.

"It's hard to put it into words" Charlotte began. "You see, I'm not sure it's deliberate. But he gives me the creeps. He stands too close to people, especially the women, and you get the feeling he's eyeing you up and down. And he's... well... patronising. The way he talks to you, it's as though he thinks he's *so superior* and the rest of us are just morons. It's almost as though he wants to pat you on the head and say 'Run along now, and leave this clever stuff to me.' Does that make sense?"

The Office Manager was concerned. "Is there anything else that makes you feel uncomfortable?"

"Well, his jokes can be pretty crude to be honest. I try not to take any notice, but I know Mel gets quite embarrassed."

As Charlotte spoke, a picture emerged of a person who was very good at the technical aspects of his job, but whose attitude was disrespectful, and who lacked the interpersonal skills to behave appropriately towards his colleagues.

The Office Manager went and spoke to Doug. "I don't know what you mean!" he protested. "Tom's great, he always delivers what we ask for, and on time too. I've never noticed him upsetting anybody."

Doug hadn't picked up on the atmosphere within the team and was reluctant to do anything about Tom's attitude. Tom was making good progress on the projects he was allocated, and seemed chirpy enough in his interactions with the others in the section. Doug shrugged it off; Tom got results and that was what he was paid for. At the end of the probationary period, Doug gave Tom a glowing review.

Charlotte was transferred to another department and no more was said about Tom's behaviour for a while. Then one day Doug received a phone call from the MD who was incandescent. He'd received a letter from a key supplier making a formal complaint about Tom's behaviour. Apparently Tom had made suggestive comments to one of their female members of staff and patted her on the bottom.

Pointing out that Tom was very good at the technical aspects of his role didn't cut any ice with the MD, who ranted about the company's reputation and valuable relationships with their suppliers. "There's more to performance than just turning in the numbers!" he raged. "You've got to know how to behave towards other people as well! He's got to go, do you hear me? Deal with it!"

As Tom had passed his probationary period, Doug had to go through a formal disciplinary process. It was all very time-consuming and unpleasant. He felt rather battered by the time it was all over. And then he had to face starting the whole recruitment process all over again.

At home over dinner, he told his wife all about it. He was expecting some sympathy, but she just said she'd come across sleazy characters like Tom herself, and it wasn't acceptable.

"People aren't like machines, you know, Doug. They need to fit into the team and get on with their colleagues. Behaviours and attitudes are just as important as technical ability."

And Doug had to concede that his wife was right – as usual.

**Learning Point 14**

*When judging a new employee's performance, you need to pay attention to their "soft skills" (communication, interacting with others, showing respect etc.) as well as their qualifications and technical competence.*

*It's not just* ***what*** *people achieve, but* ***how*** *they achieve it, that matters. Sometimes people can achieve good results in the short term, by inappropriate means such as bullying their colleagues or taking advantage of clients; but in the end the chickens will come home to roost.*

*For example, a salesperson may persuade a distributor to purchase more products than they can reasonably expect to sell. In the short term this results in brilliant sales figures, but it won't be too long before the distributor stops ordering because of the excessive stock they are holding, and their resentment of the salesperson (and by association the company itself) for putting them in that situation may lead them to stop dealing with the company altogether.*

*So the manner in which the results are achieved is just as important as the results themselves.*

*If somebody complains about one of your staff, don't be too quick to shrug it off. If they are upsetting people inside the organisation, it's quite possible they may be upsetting clients too.*

## Chapter 15: How to ensure a happy ending...

By now you will have realised that recruitment is not something that comes naturally and which you can approach with "a wing and a prayer". There are myriad pitfalls that you need to avoid at every stage of the process. Like so many other business activities, it requires adherence to the "6 P's" principle: Proper Planning Prevents Particularly Poor Performance.

Here's a step by step summary of how to go about it.

1. Ask yourself whether you need to recruit at all. Can you redistribute the tasks the previous incumbent was doing among the remaining team members? If not, is there somebody in the business already who would relish a promotion or even a sideways move? If you can fill a vacancy internally, and thereby broaden the experience of an existing employee, it may be the best option.

2. If you do need to recruit externally, write a job description or update the existing one, ensuring you focus not just on the tasks that need doing, but the overall *purpose* of the role, and the key relationships (both internally and externally) that the job holder will have to forge.

3. Then, write a person specification which lays out the essential and desirable attributes that the ideal candidate will possess. Avoid any stereotyping as regards age, gender, race, marital status etc. Focus instead on any necessary qualifications, knowledge, skills, experience, and personal attributes and aptitudes (like attention to detail, an outgoing

personality or the ability to cope well under pressure) the candidate will need to ensure success in the role.

4. Research the remuneration package to ensure that what you are offering will attract the calibre of candidates you want. You can't get a quart out of a pint pot. If your budget doesn't stretch to the "going rate" for the job, you will have to compromise on something, be that your expectations of the candidate, or the hours of work, or something else.

5. Once you've done all this preparation, the advert will be easy to write. Typically you will say a few words about the company, the job, the person you are looking for, the package, and how to apply. Place the advert in an appropriate place – be it a specialist website, the local paper, the local college, or even the newsagent's window. The right place to advertise will depend on the role and where the right candidates are going to look. Finance Directors will not go to Job Centre Plus to find their next role!

6. If you are using a recruitment agency, select one that specialises in the kind of vacancy you have, or that really understands your business and can be trusted to do a good screening job for you. Use the preparation you have done to create a very clear brief for the agency, and take into account any comments they may have on the package you're offering, as they will have a good feel for the "going rate" and the availability of good candidates.

7. When screening applications, have the advert in front of you to remind you of what you have asked for. Don't judge success by the number of applications, it

is the quality of the responses that matters. Create three piles: Yes, No and Maybe. If you have stipulated that a particular skill, qualification or level of experience is *essential*, then people who don't match up should be placed in the No pile. Then walk away from the applications and have another look at your Yes and Maybe piles the next day – or get somebody else to do so.

8. Plan your interview strategy. Will somebody else be interviewing alongside you? If so, agree who will ask which questions, so you come across as well-prepared. Use the WASP model:

    - Welcome
    - Ask Questions
    - Supply Information
    - Part Company

    Draw up a list of questions designed to probe the relevant areas – being careful to ensure that none of them could be interpreted as discriminatory. Start with open questions to get the person talking, and then use closed questions to drill down to specific facts. Follow through until you are satisfied you have got to the nitty-gritty details – don't accept bland statements and platitudes. Ask for examples. Consider whether there are any practical tests (e.g. activities related to the job) that you can include in the selection process.

9. Test your initial impressions and make sure you don't fall into the "halo and horns" trap of instant empathy or antipathy. Take your time to make up your mind. Remember it's what the person *can do* that matters,

not whether they share your passion for flower arranging.

10. Don't make an offer there and then. Even if you are sure the person is perfect, at least give yourself time to confer with your fellow interviewer to ensure you haven't missed something. And if in doubt, don't make an offer at all. Don't accept the best of a bad bunch. That's not good enough.

11. Once you are happy you have found the right candidate, don't waste time. Call and make a verbal offer. Then follow up very quickly with a written contract. Don't regret the second choice applicant until the first choice has verbally agreed to join you.

12. Carry out the immigration checks before they take up employment. Take a copy of their passport or other suitable documentation to prove their right to work in the UK. Start a file for that person and place all the relevant paperwork in it. Make a diary note of their start date and any other important dates, including the date of their end of probation review.

13. Prepare for the person's arrival: organise a "welcome pack" of useful information, get their workstation ready, sort out IT and/or other equipment, allocate a "buddy" to meet and greet the person and show them round on their first day. Plan their induction training – covering things like where the facilities are, what to do in the event of fire, where to find essential supplies, and where to find the organisation's key policies and procedures.

14. Monitor the person's performance and conduct during the probationary period. Meet with the person regularly to ensure that (a) they are settling in happily, and (b) that they are clear about what they are required to do. Prepare an End of Probation Review form identifying what they need to have mastered by that time, and provide support and training as necessary to help them get there. Seek feedback from others and take note of any concerns.

15. Don't let the date for the end of probation review slide; hold the meeting on (or before) the due date, and deliver your assessment clearly and with conviction. If they are doing well and you are pleased with their progress, take the opportunity to offer praise and encouragement. If you have concerns, don't shy away from articulating them. If needs be, extend the probationary period to allow the person to address those concerns. If you have monitored and met with the person regularly, there should not be any nasty surprises.

16. If the person is obviously not working out, and the situation cannot be turned round despite training and support, act swiftly to terminate their employment. Then ask yourself *why* it didn't work out, to help you avoid another disappointment next time. Making mistakes is only ok if you learn from them.

No recruitment process is foolproof, but if you do all this, you will maximise your chances of a happy ending. Good luck!